S0-BSD-127

T H E
Old Photographs
S E R I E S

IN THE
SOMERSET HILLS
BERNARDSVILLE, FAR HILLS AND
PEAPACK-GLADSTONE

FRANKLIN COUNTY LIBRARY SYSTEM
1 NORTH MAIN STREET
CHAMBERSBURG PA 17201

RAGGED EDGE LIBRARY
35 RAGGED EDGE RD
CHAMBERSBURG PA 17201

A bird's-eye view of Gladstone, looking north. (Norman Welsh)

THE

Old Photographs

SERIES

IN THE
SOMERSET HILLS

BERNARDSVILLE, FAR HILLS AND
PEAPACK-GLADSTONE

Compiled by
Joan M. Williams

**ALAN
SUTTON**

BATH • AUGUSTA • RENNES

First published 1994
Copyright © Joan M. Williams, 1994

ISBN 0 7524 0078 9

Published by Alan Sutton, Inc., Augusta, Maine.
Distributed by Berwick Publishing, Inc.,
1 Washington Street, Dover, New Hampshire 03820.
Printed in Great Britain by Redwood Books, Trowbridge.

Congresswoman Millicent Fenwick's pipe. The press dubbed Mrs. Fenwick "the pipe-smoking grandmother of Congress." (*The Bernardsville News*)

Contents

Acknowledgments

So many people searched through boxes and albums of pictures, then allowed me to borrow their irreplaceable photographs. They told me stories and gave me valuable insights into their towns' histories. To all of you, I give heartfelt thanks for your unstinting cooperation and enthusiasm.

To the ladies of the Bernardsville Library Local History Room who granted me access to their large picture file and so willingly found answers to my questions—Martha Dodd, Jean Hill, Eileen Johnston, Marion Kennedy, and Hilda Poole—I am grateful. Also thanks, posthumously, to Edward S. Spinning for the use of his large picture collection now in the Local History Room.

Then there were the individuals who loaned me photographs and helped identify faces in archival photos: Archie Beiser; Charles Zavalick of *The Bernardsville News*; Kim Chatfield; Harold Chesson; Anna Dubus; Hugh Fenwick; Oliver Filley; Jean, Homer, and David Hill; T. Leonard Hill; Nancy Marsh; David Neill; Daniel Ricco; Kenneth B. Schley, Jr.; Helen Smith and John D. Smith, Jr.; Marion Turner; Grace Vallachi; Evelyn Savage of the Visiting Nurse Association; and Norman Welsh.

This book would not have been possible without all of you. Thank you.

References

Among the Blue Hills … Bernardsville … A History. Bernardsville, New Jersey: Bernardsville History Book Committee, 1973.

Tutton, Jacqueline. *A Journey Through Peapack and Gladstone*. Peapack-Gladstone, New Jersey: The Friends of the Peapack-Gladstone Library, 1993.

Introduction

Difficult as it may be to imagine the Somerset Hills when horse-drawn carriages waited at railroad stations and Route 202 was a dirt road, when Borough Hall was a mill and Peapack Pond a mill race; that is the way it was.

I hope that this book will be a nostalgic trip for those who remember "the good old days," and, for the younger generation, a look at how it was back then. I also hope the photographs will bring others as much enjoyment as I have had gathering this representative collection.

It would be wonderful if this look at the past through the lens of the camera could include the Lenni Lenape Indians, who welcomed the early settlers to what we know as Bernardsville, Far Hills, and Peapack-Gladstone. Barring that, we have to be satisfied with beginning in the 1800s, when the three towns were governed by Bernards Township, as were today's Basking Ridge and Liberty Corner.

Bernardsville was originally called Vealtown, which was a little settlement around Olcott Square. Slowly Vealtown expanded as far as the present Borough Hall. Roderick Mitchell, postmaster for Vealtown (but he had to pick up the mail in Basking Ridge, the official mailing address), for some reason objected to the name "Vealtown" and campaigned successfully to have it changed to "Bernardsville" in 1840.

In the late 1800s the Mountain Colony added a new dimension to the town. Wealthy New Yorkers found the lovely rolling hills of Bernardsville to their liking and started building mansions there. Workers were imported, many of them stonemasons and gardeners from Italy who congregated in the area still known affectionately as "Little Italy."

As Bernardsville grew, so did discussion about separating from Bernards Township. In 1924 the discussion became reality and the Borough of Bernardsville was incorporated.

The Far Hills area was settled in the 1880s when E.H. Schley, a broker and realtor, came looking for land for his clients who wanted homes that provided easy access to fox-hunting. The Somerset Hills were perfect for this, and soon mansions were built.

Mr. Schley's brother, Grant B. Schley, moved out from New York in 1887. Since he, and others, needed to commute to New York, a railroad station was deemed necessary. In 1890 Grant Schley was influential in having the Delaware, Lackawanna and Western Railroad extended from Bernardsville to Peapack, with a stop convenient to Mr. Schley. As for a name for the new station, it is said that Mrs. Schley looked out at the distant hills and suggested "Far Hills." Mr. Schley also provided the town with the Far Hills Fairgrounds.

In 1921 the residents of the town voted to secede from Bernards Township and it became the Borough of Far Hills.

Peapack and Gladstone, locally known as P-G, was part of The Peapack Patent which was purchased from the Dutch in 1701. East of the village is an area called "O-Wan-A-Massie" by the Indians. It soon became known by its translation, "Pleasant Valley." Zachariah Smith settled here, as did his descendants, who made the area famous for the Smith Family Picnics, which at times had as many as one thousand attendees.

Since fox-hunting was one of the attractions that brought New Yorkers to the Somerset Hills, the Essex Fox Hounds made their headquarters in Peapack. They began sponsoring a "Farmer's Day Race Meeting" in 1910 to honor the farmers on whose lands they hunted. Five years later the New Jersey Hunt Cup was inaugurated, and it continues today as one of the oldest steeplechases in the United States.

When the railroad was extended to Peapack in 1890, the upper end of the village acquired its own post office. "Gladstone" was suggested as a name, and William Hillard, a local judge and admirer of then British Prime Minister William E. Gladstone, wrote to the prime minister and received permission to use his name.

In 1912 the twin villages voted to secede from Bedminster Township and, together, they were incorporated as the Borough of Peapack and Gladstone, variously referred to as Pea-Glad, Glad-Pack, and P-G.

The towns have grown, the dirt roads have been paved, the railroad has been electrified, and some of the mansions are gone; but the beauty of the Somerset Hills remains.

I dedicate this book to those who made the towns what they are today: the first settlers, the tradesmen and the teachers, the millers and the smiths, the Mountain Colony and Little Italy, the farmers and the huntsmen; all those who came before. You are not forgotten.

Joan M. Williams
August 1994

One
Bernardsville

Waiting for the "Millionaire's Express," *c.* 1907. Carriages await the arrival of the Mountain Colony businessmen from New York City. (Bernardsville Library Local History Room)

The Bunn Mill, *c.* 1880, along the present Mine Brook Road (Route 202). The large stone mill is now the Borough Hall and Police Headquarters. (Jean and Homer Hill)

Thomas G. and Wilma Bunn at the Bunn residence, in the late 1800s. (Bernardsville Library Local History Room)

Probably members of the Bunn family, *c.* 1900. (Bernardsville Library Local History Room)

The Bunn Mill in the early 1900s. James E. Ballantine and Thomas Bunn are next to the "up and down" saw. A large circular saw was at the right. (Bernardsville Library Local History Room)

The Old Stone Hotel (right), now Freddy's, and a barn (left), built by John Bunn in 1849. This 1889 photograph of what is now Olcott Square shows the public pump, lower center. Mr. Edward Spinning remembered carrying buckets of water from the pump to the Anderson Road School. (Bernardsville Library Local History Room)

View from Prospect Street, late 1890s. Looking down toward Morristown Road and Olcott Square (to the left), Anderson Hill can be seen in the distance. (Bernardsville Library Local History Room)

East of New Street, now Prospect Street, in the late 1800s. The H. Guehrity house is at the left and the Phillips house, now 14 Mt. Airy Road, in the center. The Baird house, now 10 Mt. Airy Road, is on the right. (Bernardsville Library Local History Room)

Looking north from Page's Hill on what is now Route 202. The Far Hills Country Day School would be on the left. (Bernardsville Library Local History Room)

The entrance to Millicent Fenwick's home on Mendham Road looked rather different back in December 1909. (Hugh Fenwick)

Lindabury Park, *c.* 1914. Its setting next to Borough Hall was slightly more rural in those days. (Anna Dubus)

The Bernards Inn, *c.* 1905. (Bernardsville Library Local History Room)

Bernardsville Mill, Mill Lane, *c.* 1890. Now Mill Street, the lane ended at the mill until it was extended to a new street, Claremont Road. (Bernardsville Library Local History Room)

A hook and ladder truck, the town's first piece of fire equipment, in front of the Old Stone Hotel's barn, *c.* 1900. Harry Wright was driving Ben Townsend's team with Dr. F.C. Sutphen (or possibly Steve Thompson), seated at the rear of the truck. Standing are: Edward Spinning, Leland Mitchell with the horse, Ben Townsend holding the two horses with the carriages, and Dan Ferrin. (Bernardsville Library Local History Room)

L.H. Nuse's blacksmith shop, 1890. Louis (Grandpa) Nuse is third from the left. (Jean and Homer Hill)

Calvin D. Smith's store, Olcott Square and Mt. Airy Road, c. 1903. (Bernardsville Library Local History Room)

Calvin D. Smith and William McMurtry's store, next to the present library, *c.* 1915. From left: Edward Amerman, Frank P. Bowman, Charles Quimby, and Calvin D. Smith. Sitting on the porch next to the store are Mrs. Smith with Willars and Theron. (Bernardsville Library Local History Room)

The Wright blacksmith shop, on Mine Brook Road between Quimby Lane and the brook, c. 1889. The Wright home is at the extreme left on the corner of Claremont Road. From left: Lambert Kagan, John Wright, Lulu Wright, Austin Wright, and Mr. and Mrs. Matthew Ryan. (Bernardsville Library Local History Room)

Bernardsville National Bank (left) and David Buist's store on Claremont Road, c. 1910. (David Neill)

Gianquitti's store, c. 1922. From left: Steven Corrado(?); Elizabeth Morrow, bookkeeper; "Pop" Gianquitti; and Anthony Gianquitti. (Bernardsville Library Local History Room)

Opposite the present library, Mine Brook Road, *c.* 1910. The Misses Petty, who made ladies' hats, and George Pepper pose with an unidentified young man. (David Neill)

Liddy Brothers' store. From left: Frank Liddy, Thomas Liddy Jr., unknown, ? Cavanaugh, Mary Liddy, Martin Liddy, unknown, and unknown. (Bernardsville Library Local History Room)

Bernardsville National Bank, *c.* 1916. (Norman Welsh)

Golf clubhouse, *c.* 1906. (Anna Dubus)

The Bernardsville Hotel, now known as "Freddy's." (David Neill)

The Claremont Hotel, 1906. The hotel, opposite the railroad station, now houses The Station restaurant. (Anna Dubus)

Somerset Inn on Mendham Road. The inn was popular with vacationing New Yorkers from 1872 until 1908, when it burned down. (Bernardsville Library Local History Room)

Somerset Inn after the fire in 1908. (David Neill)

The first Methodist Church and Parsonage at Wesley Avenue and Church Street, *c.* 1907. (Anna Dubus)

The Congregational Church, Bernardsville, *c.* 1916. Now the home of Congdon-Overlook Lodge No. 163, F & AM, it is next to the old railroad station and opposite the library. (Norman Welsh)

The men who built the new Methodist Church at Wesley Avenue and Church Street, *c.* 1913. From left: ? Moreneso, John Dick, unknown, Art Monaco, Martin Monaco, Ben Capice, unknown, unknown, unknown, and Biggio Manto. Behind and to the right of John Dick is Andy Dick. The man with the cap in the back row is John Cavaluzzo, and in front of him is ? Abbondanzo. (Nancy Marsh)

Bernardsville Library, famous for the Library Ghost, *c.* 1907. In Revolutionary days, the library was Captain John Parker's Vealtown Tavern. Phyllis, the captain's daughter, fell in love with young Dr. Byram, who roomed at the tavern. The doctor was identified as a spy, tried, and summarily hanged. During the night the coffin holding his body was brought back to the tavern for burial in the morning. Hours later, the ripping of boards, then screams of anguish, were heard. Phyllis was found, insane, beside the opened coffin. Since then, Phyllis is said to haunt the building. (Bernardsville Library Local History Room)

The first Bernards Library Association, in the early 1900s. (Bernardsville Library Local History Room)

Clara Ormiston. Miss Ormiston came to help at the library in 1918, then remained as librarian for forty-five years. (Bernardsville Library Local History Room)

Bernardsville railroad station, *c.* 1901. The building was later moved to Mine Brook Road opposite the library to become the offices of *The Bernardsville News*. (Jean and Homer Hill)

Engine No. 21, the Watsessing, at the railroad station in the late 1880s. Albert Bunn, engineer, stands proudly by his engine. (Bernardsville Library Local History Room)

The early Italian settlement in Bernardsville, c. 1906–1910. (Visiting Nurse Association)

Cheerful young ladies, c. 1912. From left: (seated) Anna Meigh, Bertha Frost, unknown, Mary Frost, Martha Dobbs Frost, and an unidentified baby; (standing) unknown, Grace Higgins, unknown, and unknown. (Jean and Homer Hill)

Colonel Post in his carriage. (Kim Chatfield)

Ladies Social Union, forerunner of The Women's Club, in 1912. From left: (top row) Mrs. Lou Nuse, Mrs. C. Allshesky, Mrs. Kuhnhardt, Mrs. DeBow, Mrs. Meseroll, Mrs. Hight, Mrs. Donohue, Mrs. Puff, Mrs. Watson Allen, Mrs. Tunison, Mrs. Adair, unknown, Mrs. Griffith, Mrs. Lent, and Mrs. Bowers; (middle row) Mrs. Shinn, Mrs. Browne, Mrs. Joe Dobbs, Mrs. F. Allshesky, Mrs. Brookens, Mrs. Dayton, and Mrs. Bennett; (sitting) Mrs. Conklin and Mrs. Sutphen. (Bernardsville Library Local History Room)

The Capice family, 1910. From left: Charles, Benedette, Carmine, Grace, Rose, and Philip. (Nancy Marsh)

Charles Philip Capice, c. 1932. (Nancy Marsh)

Mrs. Millicent Fenwick signs the register as she begins her term in the New Jersey Assembly in 1970. Senator John Ewing (right) and an unidentified official watch. Noted for her honesty and integrity, she was immortalized as Lacey Davenport in the "Doonesbury" comic strip. (*The Bernardsville News*)

Millicent Fenwick's home in 1909 with horse and carriage out front. (Hugh Fenwick)

Ogden Hammond, former US ambassador to Spain, holds his daughter Millicent (Fenwick) while her sister Mary supervises, 1910. (Hugh Fenwick)

Millicent Fenwick's parents, Mary Stevens Hammond and Ogden H. Hammond, flank Ogden's mother, Sophie Wolfe Hammond, 1910. (Hugh Fenwick)

A pensive Caroline Talmage Jelke on her wedding day in 1924. Edward Talmage III was her page, and Mary Grafton Filley her flower girl. Mary wears her grandmother's Irish lace dress. (Oliver D. Filley, Jr.)

The Filley family at Upton Pyne cottage, c. 1928. From left: Mary Grafton Filley, Mary Pyne Filley, Oliver D. Filley, Sr., and Oliver D. Filley, Jr. After Filley's death in 1961, Mary Pyne Filley married C. Suydam Cutting. (Oliver D. Filley, Jr.)

Mrs. Clarence Blair Mitchell, first president of the Visiting Nurse Association, c. 1906. The first visiting nurse was sponsored by St. Bernard's Episcopal Church of Bernardsville, but it was found that she would be more welcome if she were not connected to the church. Mrs. Mitchell then chaired a committee to direct the nurses' activities, and that committee was incorporated in 1906 as the Visiting Nurse Association of Bernardsville with Mrs. Mitchell as president. (Visiting Nurse Association)

The surgery at the Visiting Nurse Association headquarters in Bernardsville, c. 1923. Patients were relieved of troublesome tonsils and adenoids at Visiting Nurse clinics in Peapack and Bernardsville. After surgery, patients rested in the recovery room, pictured below. (Visiting Nurse Association)

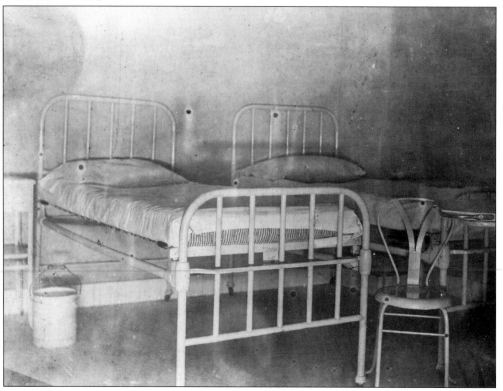

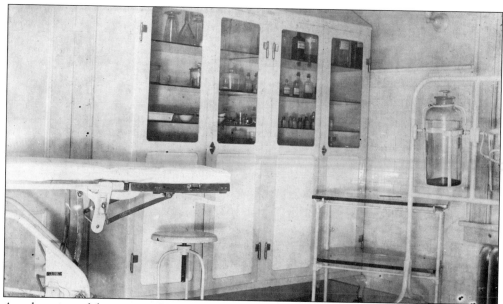

Another view of the surgery. (Visiting Nurse Association)

Visiting Nurses' transportation in 1906. (Visiting Nurse Association)

Visiting Nurses and their new transportation, *c.* 1914. (Visiting Nurse Association)

July Fourth parade, 1905. The Vealtown Brigade with their up-to-date firefighting equipment. (Bernardsville Library Local History Room)

The Fire Company's chemical engine, 1905. Driver Fred Ehrich reins in David Buist's team, Prince and Duke. (Bernardsville Library Local History Room)

Joseph Dobbs, chief of the Fire Company in 1915/16. (Bernardsville Library Local History Room)

Fire Company chief Sanford W. Lewison, 1908. (Bernardsville Library Local History Room)

Bernardsville Fire Company at attention in 1909. From left: John McWilliams, chief; Harry J. Davis, assistant chief; William J. Lyon, chief warden; I.N. Bowers; Kenneth McKenzie; Thomas Parry; George T. Pepper; John E. Puff; A.B. Gibb; Thomas Liddy; Joseph Dobbs; Fred Compton; Dr. R.E. Mosedale; Frank Van Orden; W.E. Bunn; C.H. Griffith; Horace McWilliams; Charles Alpaugh; Dr. F.C. Sutphen; Dr. L.E. Tuttle; L.H. Nuse; Theron B. Smith; Rev. T.A. Conover; Seeley Palmer; Harry Wright; and Fred Ehrich, driver. (Bernardsville Library Local History Room)

Edward S. Spinning, *c.* 1918. Mr. Spinning was Fire Company chief from 1917 to 1919. (Bernardsville Library Local History Room)

Tommy Dorsey poses in "his" engine, *c.* 1939. He was named honorary chief of the Fire Company when he lived on Old Army Road between 1935 and 1939. (Bernardsville Library Local History Room)

The old schoolhouse on Mine Brook Road. After the school was closed, it was moved to the back of the Willoughby property on Mine Brook Road. (*The Bernardsville News*)

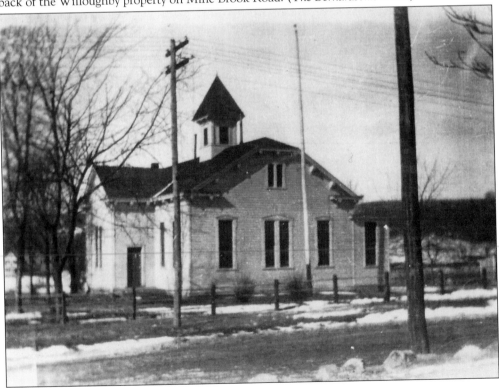

Anderson Road school, c. 1885. The building was the first Methodist Church in Bernardsville, then used as a school in the early 1880s. From left: (first row) Mamie Stinson, unknown, Ella Rundio, Lulu Wright, Bessie Taylor, unknown, unknown, unknown, and Ella Conway; (second row) unknown, Fred Ballentine, Joseph Lowery, Stephen Riel, Willars Smith, Bert Apgar, Theron Smith, J. Rooney, George Thorpe (teacher), Charles Quimby, James Allen, Mary Riel, Bertha Rundio, Minnie Wolfe, Mamie Thompson, Stella Abel, Ada Allen, Mary Liddy, and May Apgar; (third row) John Rogers, unknown, unknown, John Fitzpatrick, unknown, unknown, unknown, Will Lowery, Earl Bunn, unknown, Leland Mitchell, Edward Spinning, Frank Blazure, unknown, Bentley Amerman, and unknown. (Bernardsville Library Local History Room)

Opposite: Methodist Church, Anderson Road, c. 1880. Shortly after 1880, the building was converted to a school when a new church was built at the junction of Wesley Avenue and Church Street. (Anna Dubus)

Somerset Inn School, *c.* 1900. A converted icehouse served as a school for the children of Somerset Inn employees and some local youngsters. (Bernardsville Library Local History Room)

Somerset Inn School, *c.* 1900, from a student's perspective. (Bernardsville Library Local History Room)

Mine Brook School, c. 1898. The young boy with the bow in the middle of the first row is William Irving Frost. His sister, Bertha Frost, is the tall girl third from the left in the next to the top row. (Jean and Homer Hill)

Kindergarten class at the Anderson Road School, c. 1910. From left: (top row) Christine Trumball (teacher), Anna Dubus, Mary Cirillo, Mary Doherty, Louise Mattai, Susan Lucas, Ella Fried, and Lucy Gardner; (center) Liz Parr; (middle row) Violet Lindsey, Rose Jaeger, Elizabeth Ruetter, Agnes Doherty, Mary Foldi, Julia Riccardi, Bessie ?, Lillian Pearson, and Tillie Ganji; (bottom row) Clifford Ludlow, unknown, unknown, unknown, Emilio Molinaro, Carl Riccardi, unknown, unknown, unknown, unknown, Stephan Budvanski, and Joseph Zarhardt. (Anna Dubus)

Second grade class, c. 1910. Mr. Meserale, principal, and Miss Larkin, teacher, stand at the back of the room. Michael Dubus is in the next to last seat in the far left row. (Anna Dubus)

Olcott School, 1905. The horse-drawn "states" could be bringing high school students from Liberty Corner (they were picked up at the Basking Ridge Presbyterian Church), or perhaps they are setting out on an excursion. (Jean and Homer Hill)

Grammar School students at the Olcott building, 1907. (David Neil)

Bernards High School Orchestra, 1916. (Bernardsville Library Local History Room)

Eighth grade class at the Olcott building, 1910. (David Neill)

Bernards High School graduating class, c. 1913. The group is gathered on the steps of the stucco school building that was used as the high school between 1912 and 1915. It was razed in 1967. (Jean and Homer Hill)

Charles Alpaugh driving political candidates, probably to a rally, *c.* 1910. (Anna Dubus)

The Sons of Italy parade, 1921. (David Neill)

RAGGED EDGE LIBRARY
35 RAGGED EDGE RD
CHAMBERSBURG PA 17201

John Puff and Peter Miller at the July Fourth parade in 1905. (Bernardsville Library Local History Room)

The July Fourth parade in 1905 entering the Polo Grounds. (Bernardsville Library Local History Room)

The Bernards High School Band marches down Mt. Airy Road over the railroad tracks in 1947. The parade celebrated the fiftieth anniversary of the Bernardsville Fire Company. (Bernardsville Library Local History Room)

The Boy Scouts also marched in honor of the Fire Company's fiftieth anniversary in 1947. (Bernardsville Library Local History Room)

The first prize float in the July Fourth parade of 1940. It was said that there were no roses left in town after the float was decorated by: (from left) Grace Capice, Bette Hoare, Mary De Fillipis, and Agnes Dupay. (Grace Vallachi)

A July Fourth parade in the 1920s. Philip Capice is driving his truck, which was decorated by the ladies. Rafaela Carrado Gianquitti is sitting in the back, fourth from the right. (Nancy Marsh)

Parade watchers in this 1940s photograph included Harold Dobbs, center, holding a child. (Bernardsville Library Local History Room)

Mr. and Mrs. Gianquitti next to a tree felled by the hurricane of October 1938. (Bernardsville Library Local History Room)

A gathering of The Sons of Italy, c. 1940s. From left: (top row) Sylvester Molinaro, unknown, unknown, unknown, unknown, Albert Pistilli (Mike Ricciardi in front of him), Dominick Tongno, Joseph De Reinzo, A.J. Maddaluna, Larry Gianetti, Joseph Latino, Carl Ricciardi, Dominick Spagnalo, Joseph Di Norcia, Sarge ?, Salvatore Pistilli, and Philip Capice; (middle row) Joseph Ricciardi, Mike Florio, William Ricciardi, Albert Zanengo, ? Albino, Ralph Martucci, Frank Mastrobattista, Carmine Petriccione, Frank Tullo, Sisto ?, ? Diamino, Salvatore Balsamello, Frank Russo, Angelo Molinaro, Steve ?, Angelo Cavaluzzo, Benedette Capice, Frank Treppiccione, unknown, Angelo Morene, Louis Andiorio, and Louis Matero; (bottom row) Josephine Pistilli, Mrs. Joseph Bocchino, Stephanie Maddaluna, Mrs. Joseph Matteo, Mrs. Salvatore Balsamello, Mrs. Vincent Balsamello, unknown, Mrs. Joseph Nardone, Mrs. Martucci, unknown, unknown, unknown, and Angelina Capice. (Nancy Marsh)

Opposite: Downtown Bernardsville awash in the flood of August 23, 1942. (Bernardsville Library Local History Room)

International Order of Odd Fellows, 1915. From left: (top row) Martin Monaro, Joseph Hamilton, Charles ?, William ?, and unknown; (bottom row) Charles Whitcomb, unknown, and Samuel Puff. (Bernardsville Library Local History Room)

Ladies of the Order of the Eastern Star, April 9, 1942. From left: (top row) Lena B. Bartles (jr. past matron), Susie E. Sutphen (past matron and installing chaplain), and Audrey G. Florio (past matron, marshall); (middle row) Louise Van Varick (warder), Elizabeth Pantly (Electa), Settimia Nervine (Martha), Pauline Kolody (Ruth), Mary Shaw (installing matron), Mary S. Paine (Esther), Edna M. Beatty (Adah), Ruth Kraus (organist), Mabel S. Lance (assoc. warder); (seated) Anna M. Anderson (chaplain), Nellie B. Garrabrant (treasurer), Margaret G. Pope (conductress), Mae B. Welsh (W.M.), E.S. Spinning (W.P. Pro Tem), Grace A. Howes (assoc. matron), Marion Bailey (assoc. conductress), and Margaret Wunder (secretary). (Bernardsville Library Local History Room)

Two

Far Hills

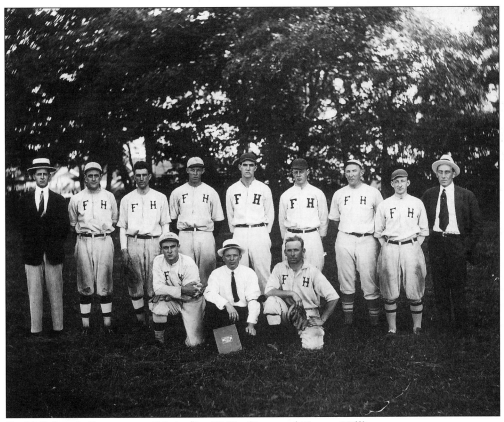

Far Hills baseball team, possibly in the 1940s. (Jean and Homer Hill)

Dumont Road, looking toward the ball field. Ludlow's Market is on the right. (Norman Welsh)

Far Hills School, *c.* 1916. (Norman Welsh)

Grantly Country Club, *c.* 1916. D'Apolito's Tailor Shop is now at this site. (Norman Welsh)

Union Hook and Ladder Company No. 1, *c.* 1916. (Norman Welsh)

Hub Mill, Far Hills, c. 1890. (Helen Smith)

Mine Brook station, *c.* 1908. A bucolic setting for the tiny railroad station which was just off Whitenack Road between Bernardsville and Far Hills. (Jean and Homer Hill)

Opposite: St. Elizabeth Church on Peapack Road, Far Hills, *c.* 1916. (Norman Welsh)

The wreck of the 7:42 p.m. at Far Hills on August 3, 1908. (Bernardsville Library Local History Room)

Far Hills Firehouse, 1906. (Bernardsville Library Local History Room)

Attics were well searched for the costumes for the Washington's Birthday social at the Bedminster Reformed Church in 1914. From left: (seated on floor) Betty McLaughlin, Martha Flomerfelt, Martha McLaughlin, May Dowling and Mary Howard; (second row) Mildred Townley, Franklin Potter, Mr. Bockhoven, Mrs. Charles Barker, Mrs. Joseph Layton and Eleanor Nevius; (third row) Mrs. Loretta Plotts, Mrs. A. Layton Nevius, Effie Beekman, Mrs. George Potter, Mrs. David Rinehart, Mrs. John McLaughlin, Mrs. Ellis Dow, the Rev. Charles Gilbert Mallery, Mrs. Mallery, Mrs. Charles High Rogers, Mrs. Bertha Lane and A. Layton Nevius; (fourth row) Ted Stratton, Joseph Layton, Mrs. Grace Sueter, Mr. and Mrs. Rod Oakes, Mrs. P.D. Lane, Mrs. Ella Gutleber, Mabel Logan and Mrs. Harriet Wyckoff; (fifth row) John McLaughlin, Blackwell Mallery, Vernon Hall, Charles Mallery, Richard Mallery, Chauncey Oakes, Ken Paulson, Mrs. Mark Osborne, Gret Van Arsdale, Marion Elmer, Mary Frost, Eleanor Stratton, Mildred Pantley, Marion Rice and Mildred Harsell. (Jean and Homer Hill)

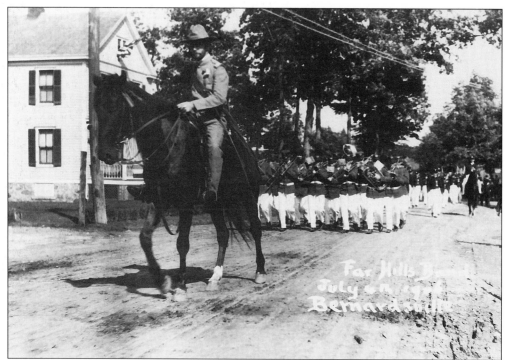

The Far Hills Band helped set the pace at the Bernardsville July Fourth parade in 1906. (Bernardsville Library Local History Room)

The brightly decorated Far Hills Hook and Ladder marched at the Bernardsville July Fourth parade in 1906. (Bernardsville Library Local History Room)

The Far Hills delegation at the Bernardsville July Fourth parade in 1906. (Bernardsville Library Local History Room)

Stone bridge on the Schley Estate, Far Hills. (Norman Welsh)

Old and new bridges at Far Hills, *c.* 1916. (Norman Welsh)

Ellen R. Schley (Mrs. Kenneth Schley, Sr.), in the late 1800s. (Kenneth B. Schley, Jr.)

Oliver D. Filley, Jr. and Mary Grafton Filley at the Essex Fox Hounds race meet in Far Hills, *c.* 1929. (Oliver D. Filley, Jr.)

Thornton Wilson, Harriet Post Wilson Welles, and Mary Pyne Filley (Cutting) at the Far Hills Fairgrounds, *c.* 1926. (Oliver D. Filley, Jr.)

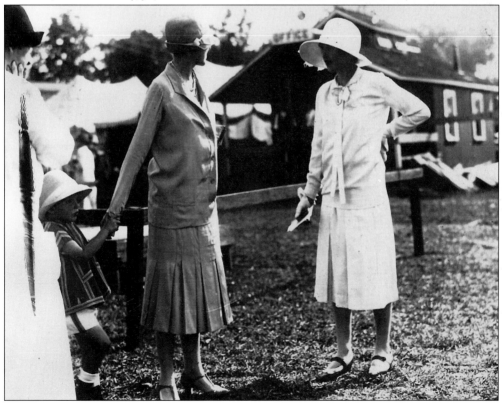

Mrs. Kenneth B. Schley, Sr. with Mr. and Mrs. Charles Scribner at the Far Hills Fairgrounds horse show in 1930. (Kenneth B. Schley, Jr.)

The Reeve Schley family posing with their dogs in the 1930s. From left: Eleanor Schley Todd (New Jersey Governor Christie Todd Whitman's mother), Reeve Schley, Sr., John P. Schley standing in front of his father, Mrs. Reeve Schley, Sr. and Reeve Schley, Jr. (Kenneth B. Schley, Jr.)

Three
Peapack and Gladstone

The wedding of Lily Bocchino and Frank Morano, *c.* 1927. The girls' bonnet-like headdresses and the men's center-part hairstyles were typical of the era. From left: (back row) Boyden Formerfelt, unknown, Daniel Ricco, Mike Salvia, Frank Morano, ? Salvia, Tony Premaco, unknown, and Charles Morano; (front row) Denny DeSesso, unknown, Fannie Ricco, unknown, Lily Bocchino Morano, Eugene Salvia, Mary Premaco, ? Bocchino, and Madeline Bocchino. (Daniel Ricco)

Looking north on Main Street, Gladstone. The Hotel Gladstone can be seen on the far left. (Harold Chesson)

The post office and the Van Arsdale and Ballentine Department Store in 1906. (Bernardsville Library Local History Room)

G.F. Hill Feedmill, *c.* 1911. (T. Leonard Hill)

G.F. Hill, John Beiser, and Will Swick pose in front of the Little Garage and Blue Barn (livery stable), *c*. 1913. (T. Leonard Hill)

The hub factory in the early 1900s. Hubs for wagon wheels were made here at Ludlow's factory in Peapack. (Bernardsville Library Local History Room)

The Smith mill and house at Hub Hollow above Ravine Lake in the 1800s. (Bernardsville Library Local History Room)

Mill wheel at Hub Hollow in the late 1800s. (Bernardsville Library Local History Room)

Theodore S. Hill's early livery business provided both closed and open transportation for hire. The closed version is shown here. (T. Leonard Hill)

This photograph shows the open version. (T. Leonard Hill)

By the 1920s, Theodore S. Hill offered a more familiar-looking taxi. (T. Leonard Hill)

Main Street, Peapack, with the post office on the left, *c.* 1920. (Norman Welsh)

Vliet's Hotel, Gladstone, possibly at the turn of the century. The ice cream wagon is labeled "E.C. Lamerson." (Kim Chatfield)

Howard House in the early 1900s. Also known as the Peapack Hotel, it was long operated as a family hotel and tavern. It was purchased by Komline-Sanderson Engineering Co. and then torn down in 1975. (Bernardsville Library Local History Room)

Hotel Gladstone, in the 1920s. It is now Chatfield's. (Bernardsville Library Local History Room)

The first telephone exchange in Peapack rang in the house on the corner of Main Street and Willow Avenue. (Kim Chatfield)

Maple Cottage, Peapack, *c.* 1909. Kate Macy Ladd opened Maple Cottage as a summer retreat and guest home for "professional and working women of refinement who were unable to pay for proper accommodations while convalescing from illness . . . or otherwise in need of rest." Later the home of the Sheptocks, the house was demolished in 1990. (Norman Welsh)

A horse-drawn tank truck waters down the dusty street in July 1907. (T. Leonard Hill)

Cutting ice on Charles Van Arsdale Smith's pond in 1936. (John D. Smith, Jr.)

A thresher, *c.* 1930. Shown but not identified are: Stewart Howell, Charles Van Arsdale Smith, and John Dayton Smith. (Helen Smith)

The last load of hay, *c.* 1925. (Helen Smith)

Liberty Park. In 1938, Liberty Park was the ol' swimmin' hole. (Archie Beiser)

Liberty Park in 1938. Is that a swan dive Stanley
Trimmer is emulating? (Archie Beiser)

Liberty Park. The hurricane of 1938 did extensive damage in the area, as evidenced in the park. (Archie Beiser)

Liberty Park. Once upon a time there were bridges, built by Paul Rasmussen in 1938, connecting the little islands to each other and to the mainland. (Archie Beiser)

A boy named Archie went fishing at Liberty Park in the 1930s, but the expedition ended when his homemade raft sank beneath him. (Archie Beiser)

Peapack-Gladstone eighth grade graduating class in 1925. From left: (top row) Pierre Hatton, Renee Ike, Paul Gallo, Margery Fenner, M. Harding (principal and eighth grade teacher, later New Jersey commissioner of education), Thomas Ward, Meredith Todd, Daniel Ricco, and unknown; (middle row) Evelyn Allen, Dorothy Kinsey, Florence ?, Evelyn (Dottie) Hill, Bertha Alpaugh, Martha Hendershot, Madeline Bocchino, and Edna Shelley; (front row) Louis Bocchino, Mary Matero, William Ballantine, Marie Pote, and Kenneth Deraney. (Daniel Ricco)

Peapack-Gladstone elementary school graduation, c. 1928. From left: (top row) unknown, unknown, unknown, unknown, unknown, Mr. Twitchell, unknown, unknown, unknown, and Frank Ginnie; (middle row) Rose DeSesso, unknown, ? Hill, unknown, Louise Bernadino, unknown, Rose Russo, unknown, Kay Lynch, and Mrs. Chadwick (teacher); (seated) unknown, unknown, and Eugene Salvia. (Daniel Ricco)

Peapack Valley Fire Company No. 1, c. 1916. (Norman Welsh)

The new chemical fire engine, c. 1910. Ed Amerman is driving, with J. Forbe Guerin (?) and J.J. Foley at the rear. (Bernardsville Library Local History Room)

Garney F. Hill with his team on the first fire engine, *c.* 1910. (Kim Chatfield)

F. Hill driving his team on the fire engine at the carnival, *c.* 1910. St. Luke's Episcopal Church is in the background. (T. Leonard Hill)

The first ambulance, in the 1930s. (Archie Beiser)

The remains of the Cleveland Laboratory. The laboratory, which made waterproof bags, burned to the ground in 1943. (Archie Beiser)

Peapack B.B.C.

Peapack baseball team. From left:
(top row) Frank Trimmer, Jess
Beavers, Tom Howard, Ed Swick,
Oscar Hill, and Bill (Willie)
Howard; (bottom row) "Scott"
Buchannon, Charles Ruhman,
John Ike, and "Gus" Ike. (Kim
Chatfield)

Reformed Church, Gladstone.
(Norman Welsh)

That's not bubble gum, that's a balloon-blowing-up contest in the 1940s. (Archie Beiser)

And then there was a baby parade. Sandra and Sarah Bayles are at the far right, with, possibly, one of the Manning boys next to them. (Archie Beiser)

Soap Box Derby, 1946. The tall fellow near the flag is Clarence Miller. Tony Orlando stands on the right with his entry "Tainter Avenue Special," and Thomas Kelly is next to him. Clyde Manning, one of the judges, is on the far right, with Bill Mayberry next to him. (Archie Beiser)

Frank Crater in his 1908 Brush horseless carriage. (Kim Chatfield)

The Gladstone station, 1908. The freight house on the left was later used as the railroad station in *The Miracle Worker*. (Bernardsville Library Local History Room)

When the train didn't stop at the end of the line. In November 1961, the brakes failed on the Gladstone train and it plowed into the house just beyond the last stop. Did the prayer meeting in progress in another room have anything to do with the lack of injuries? The house was later demolished. (David Hill)

The Gladstone trestle of the Rockaway Valley Railroad, *c*. 1900. Fondly known as the Rock-a-Bye-Baby line because of its bumpy ride, it ran through Gladstone from Oldwick to the Whippany River. (Bernardsville Library Local History Room)

These unidentified young ladies seem to have been celebrating something in the early 1930s. (T. Leonard Hill)

An unidentified family out for a ride, *c.* 1916. The flag on the hood could indicate a July Fourth outing. (Kim Chatfield)

The cart that used to carry lime from the quarry seemed a good place to pose for a photograph in the late 1800s. Anna Hill is the young lady in the sunbonnet. (T. Leonard Hill)

The very latest in personal transportation: a 1915 Chevrolet that cost $490. Standing on the left is Mrs. Ed Ludlow. (T. Leonard Hill)

Maple Avenue, looking north. (Norman Welsh)

Joseph Ricco, Daniel Ricco's father, in the uniform of the Italian Carbineri, 1905. (Daniel Ricco)

The Creatura family, in the late 1800s. From left: Lucia (Ricco), Mrs. Creatura, Michael, and Leonard. (Daniel Ricco)

The DeSesso family. Rose, standing, and Anthony, seated, pose for a family portrait with their children, Jennie on the left, John, Denny, and, on his father's lap, Angelo. (George DeSesso, born at a later date, became the druggist in town, taking over the Dubus Drugstore.) (Daniel Ricco)

The Ricco family, c. 1924. From left: Joseph, Theresa (Carnivale), John, and Angelo. (Daniel Ricco)

The wedding of Joan Capice and Daniel
Ricco, December 29, 1945. From left:
Arthur D'Ambrosia, Philip Capice,
Grace Capice Vallachi, Joan Capice
Ricco, Daniel Ricco, and Leonard Ricco.
(Daniel Ricco)

Archie and May Betton, age two and
four respectively, in 1893. (T. Leonard
Hill)

Peter Zachariah Smith in the early 1800s. (John D. Smith, Jr.)

The home of Peter Zachariah Smith, c. 1920. The original house was built in 1820, with additions made later. (John D. Smith, Jr.)

A merry miss, Marion E. Marshall, in 1905. Miss Marshall was the future Mrs. Charles Van Arsdale Smith. (Helen Smith)

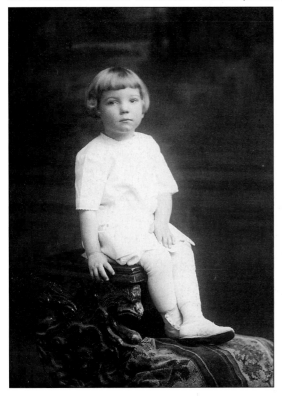

John Dayton Smith, c. 1916. (Helen Smith)

Smith Family & Friends' Re-Union
Established   1876.

The Smith Family of New Jersey in acknowledgement of their ancestral devotion, feeling grateful for the prosperity attending their general welfare, and prompted by the social and religious influences to which their fathers so strictly adhered, do hereby re-unite and form an Association for the purpose of encouraging those social qualities which should accompany every Christian body; thus, in memory of their ancestors, the decendants of John Smith and Christian Hassel, his wife, down to the seventh generation, have organized and established the Smith Family and Friends' Re-Union.

Peter Z. Smith   Abraham Smith
J. J. Smith   John D. Smith   James Smith
W. A. Smith

Smith Family and Friend's Re-Union 1877

A Smith Family Reunion, held near the Hub Mill in the late 1800s. (John D. Smith, Jr.)

Opposite: Notice of the establishment of the Smith Family Reunion, 1877. It was signed by Peter Z. Smith, Abraham Smith, Z.Z. Smith, James Smith, and W.A. Smith. (John D. Smith, Jr.)

Charles Van Arsdale Smith in the 1890s. (John D. Smith, Jr.)

Charles Van Arsdale Smith and John Dayton Smith standing, with Margery Smith in the car, c. 1920. (Helen Smith)

Main Street awash after the 1942 hurricane. Dubus Drugstore can be seen on the right. (Archie Beiser)

The Gladstone Market was reached by boat after the 1942 hurricane. (Archie Beiser)

The World War II honor roll that Archie Beiser made, and kept up to date, *c.* 1944. (Archie Beiser)

There was a lot of snow along Main Street in 1947. (Archie Beiser)

Four
Horses, Hounds, and Hunting

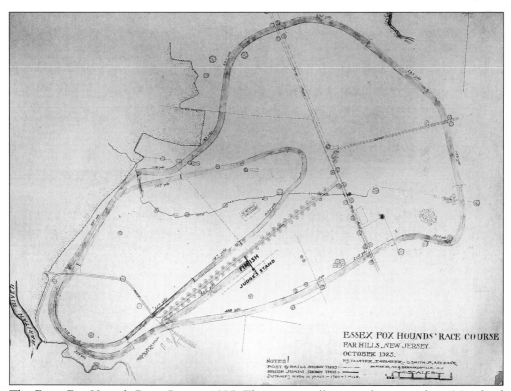

The Essex Fox Hounds Race Course, 1925. The race is still run at the same place, Moorland Farms (previously Froheim). Originally it was held by the landowners for their farmers. Today the profits from the race go to Somerset Hospital. (Kenneth B. Schley, Jr.)

Mr. and Mrs. Charles Pfizer and friends before the hunt, in the early 1900s. (Bernardsville Library Local History Room)

The Essex Fox Hounds. Kenneth B. Schley, Sr., master of the Fox Hounds, is in the lead. (Kenneth B. Schley, Jr.)

Mrs. Kenneth Schley, Sr. (Kenneth B. Schley, Jr.)

Mary Pyne Filley (Cutting) at the Far Hills Horse Show, *c.* 1928. (Oliver D. Filley, Jr.)

Edward Talmage driving Taffy in Class 16 for ponies in harness, probably at the Bernardsville Polo Grounds. (Bernardsville Library Local History Room)

At the Bernardsville Polo Grounds, in the early 1900s. A blue ribbon went to Mrs. Swan, driving for W.T. Savage (right). Miss Evelyn Schley, center, and Miss Augusta Bliss, left, also drove. (Bernardsville Library Local History Room)

An entry in the horse show at the Bernardsville Polo Grounds. (Kim Chatfield)

James C. Brady, master of the Fox Hounds; George Brice, huntsman; and Kenneth B. Schley, Sr., master of the Fox Hounds. (Kenneth B. Schley, Jr.)

Ready for the hunt at the home of Kenneth B. Schley, Sr. in Bernardsville, *c.* 1930. (Kenneth B. Schley, Jr.)

Hunting with Mr. Post's Somerset Beagles, in the early 1900s. Mr. Post and Mr. Lloyd are on the left. (Oliver D. Filley, Jr.)

Mary Pyne Filley (Cutting) and Gertrude Whitney at the Essex Hunt Club in 1927. (Oliver D. Filley, Jr.)

Mrs. Charles Pfizer calling the hounds, in the early 1900s. (Bernardsville Library Local History Room)

The Essex Fox Hounds in 1925. George Brice, huntsman, is third from the right. (Kenneth B. Schley, Jr.)

Five

Homes and Estates

Aerial view of Millicent Fenwick's home on Mendham Road, *c.* 1925. (Hugh Fenwick)

Froheim in the 1890s. Now Moorland Farms, Froheim was built by Grant B. Schley. (Kenneth B. Schley, Jr.)

The Riker residence in Peapack. (Norman Welsh)

Meadowbrook Farm, Richard V. Lindabury's residence, in 1906. (Bernardsville Library Local History Room)

Blairsden in the early 1900s. C. Ledyard Blair built his French chateau-style home overlooking Ravine Lake. The lake was formed by damming the Raritan River, and the terraced steps led down to it. (Bernardsville Library Local History Room)

Olcott Avenue before it was paved. (Norman Welsh)

The Old Stone House, located between Far Hills and Peapack. A turn-of-the-century postcard identifies it as the home of General Reeve and one of New Jersey's oldest landmarks. (Bernardsville Library Local History Room)

H.R. Hardenburgh's home, 1906. (Bernardsville Library Local History Room)

Originally the residence of James E. Hulhizer, this house later became the Eastern Star Home, and then the Stonemere Nursing Home, which burned down in April 1969. (Bernardsville Library Local History Room)

The home of J.A. Stursberg on Clark Road. (Bernardsville Library Local History Room)

George I. Seney's home on Mendham Road. (Bernardsville Library Local History Room)

A.R. Kuser, Jr.'s home. (Bernardsville Library Local History Room)

The Hunt family residence, 1906. (Bernardsville Library Local History Room)

G.R. Mosle's home, 1906. This later became the St. John the Baptist School. (Bernardsville Library Local History Room)

Blythewood, home of Henry R. Kunhardt, in the late 1800s. It was later purchased by Colonel Anthony Kuser and renamed Faircourt. (Bernardsville Library Local History Room)

Parlor at Blythewood in the late 1800s. (Bernardsville Library Local History Room)

Blythewood's gatehouse on Mountain Top and Overleigh Roads in the late 1800s. (Bernardsville Library Local History Room)

Upton Pyne, Percy R. Pyne's estate. (Bernardsville Library Local History Room)

George B. Post, Jr.'s residence, Kenilwood, c. 1906. It was briefly owned by the boxer, Mike Tyson, putting Bernardsville briefly in the national spotlight. (Bernardsville Library Local History Room)

F.P. Olcott's home on Mine Mount Road. (Bernardsville Library Local History Room)

Childs Farm, c. 1904. The residence of William Childs is in the center of the photograph. (Bernardsville Library Local History Room)

The W.S. Lawson home in Far Hills, 1906. (Benardsville Local History Room)

The home of Mrs. J. H. Ballentine in Bernardsville. (Norman Welsh)

Haley Fiske estate, 1906. (Bernardsville Library Local History Room)

The Japanese Garden on the Charles Pfizer estate, *c.* 1906. (Bernardsville Library Local History Room)

The home of Ezra and Catherine Lamoreux Dayton in the 1890s. Mr. Dayton owned the Mt. Airy Nurseries on Pill Hill Road, and named Mt. Airy Road. The house was built in 1876 on the present Dayton Crescent but is no longer standing. (David Neill)

The parlor of the Dayton home, c. 1890.

The home of Charles Dana. (Bernardsville Library Local History Room)

Forest F. Dryden's home, 1906. (Bernardsville Library Local History Room)

The A.A. Fowler residence in Peapack. (Norman Welsh)